COUNTRIES  OF THE WORLD

Manuel Alvarado

with photographs by David Cumming

Illustrated by Malcolm S. Walker

The Bookwright Press
New York • 1990

Titles in this series

Australia	Italy
Canada	Japan
The Caribbean	The Netherlands
China	New Zealand
France	Pakistan
Great Britain	Spain
Greece	The United States
India	West Germany

Cover *A Spanish coastal village.*

Opposite *The village of Albarracin, near Teruel in Aragon.*

© Copyright 1989 Wayland (Publishers) Ltd

First Published in the United States by
The Bookwright Press
387 Park Avenue South
New York NY 10016

First published in 1989 by
Wayland (Publishers) Ltd
61 Western Road, Hove
East Sussex BN3 1JD, England

Library of Congress Cataloging–in–Publication Data

Alvarado, Manuel, 1948—
  Spain / by Manual Alvarado.
    p. cm. — (Countries of the world)
  Includes bibliographical references.
  Summary: An introduction to the geography, history, government, economy, culture, and people of Spain.
  ISBN 0–531–18332–7
  1. Spain—Juvenile literature. [1. Spain.] I. Title.
II. Series: Countries of the world (New York, N.Y.)
DP17.A63 1989
946—dc20   69—36790
                                                CIP
Typeset by Rachel Gibbs, Wayland   AC
Printed in Italy by G. Canale and C.S.p.A., Turin

Contents

All words appearing in **bold** are explained in the glossary on page 46.

1 Introducing Spain

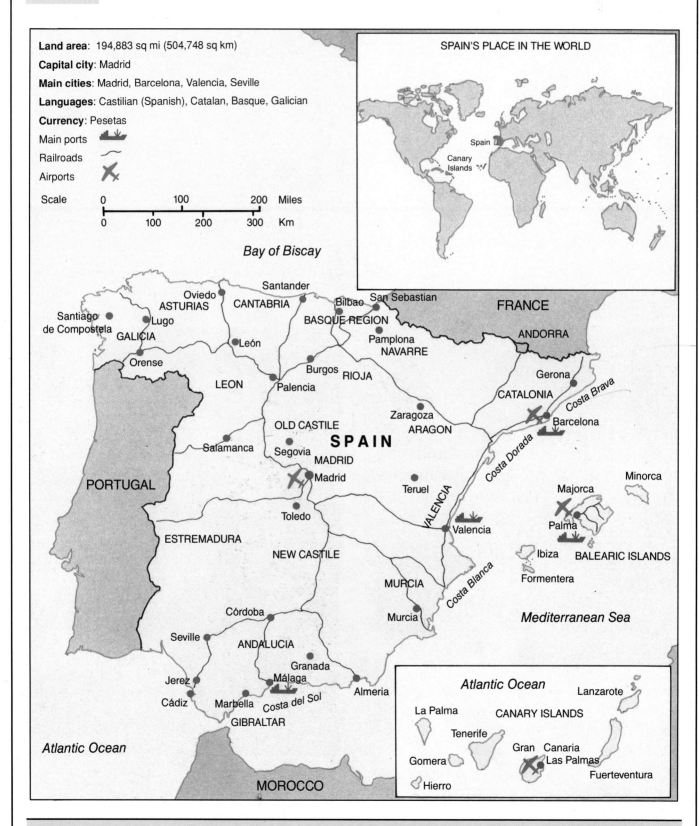

Land area: 194,883 sq mi (504,748 sq km)

Capital city: Madrid

Main cities: Madrid, Barcelona, Valencia, Seville

Languages: Castilian (Spanish), Catalan, Basque, Galician

Currency: Pesetas

Main ports

Railroads

Airports

Scale

| 0 | 100 | 200 | Miles |
| 0 | 100 | 200 | 300 | Km |

SPAIN'S PLACE IN THE WORLD

Spain

Canary
Islands

Bay of Biscay

Santander

Oviedo   CANTABRIA   Bilbao   San Sebastian   FRANCE

ASTURIAS   BASQUE REGION

Santiago
de Compostela   Lugo   Pamplona   ANDORRA

GALICIA   León   NAVARRE

Orense   Burgos   RIOJA   Gerona

LEON   Palencia   CATALONIA   Costa Brava

Zaragoza   Barcelona

OLD CASTILE   ARAGON   Costa Dorada

Salamanca   Segovia   SPAIN

MADRID

PORTUGAL   Madrid   Teruel   VALENCIA   Minorca

Majorca

Toledo   Palma

ESTREMADURA   Valencia   Ibiza   BALEARIC ISLANDS

NEW CASTILE   Formentera

Costa Blanca

MURCIA   Mediterranean Sea

Córdoba   Murcia

Seville   ANDALUCIA

Granada

Jerez   Málaga

Cádiz   Marbella   Almeria

Costa del Sol

GIBRALTAR

Atlantic Ocean

MOROCCO

Atlantic Ocean   Lanzarote

La Palma   CANARY ISLANDS

Tenerife   Gran Canaria

Gomera   Las Palmas

Hierro   Fuerteventura

Spain is the second largest country in Western Europe. It is twice the size of Italy, and four times the size of Britain. It occupies most of the land mass called the Iberian Peninsula covering an area of 194,883 sq mi (504,748 sq km). Over 40 million people live in Spain making it the fifth most populated European country.

The north coast of Spain faces the Atlantic Ocean and the Bay of Biscay, while to the east is the Mediterranean Sea. The country is cut off from the rest of Europe by the second highest mountain range in the continent – the Pyrenees – which runs along the border with France. Portugal lies to the west and Gibraltar to the south. Offshore in the Mediterranean are the Balearic Islands and to the southwest in the Atlantic are the Canary Islands.

Spain is a country with a complicated ancient history and culture. When the Spanish **Empire** was at its peak in the seventeenth and eighteenth centuries it exerted a huge influence on the rest of the world. As a result of its conquest and domination of the South American continent, nineteen countries in Latin America and the Caribbean speak Spanish as their first language. It is estimated that over 220 million people speak Spanish outside Spain, making it the second most widely spoken language in the world, after English.

In this century Spain has seen great political changes, living through civil war and an oppressive **dictatorship**. It is now modernizing its attitudes, and has a much freer **democratic** form of government.

Spain has developed tourism as one of its major industries. Hence its economy has been growing very quickly in recent years. In 1986 Spain became a member of the **European Economic Community** (EEC) and has become more involved in western and world politics.

Right A Spanish village in the Pyrenees.

2 Land and climate

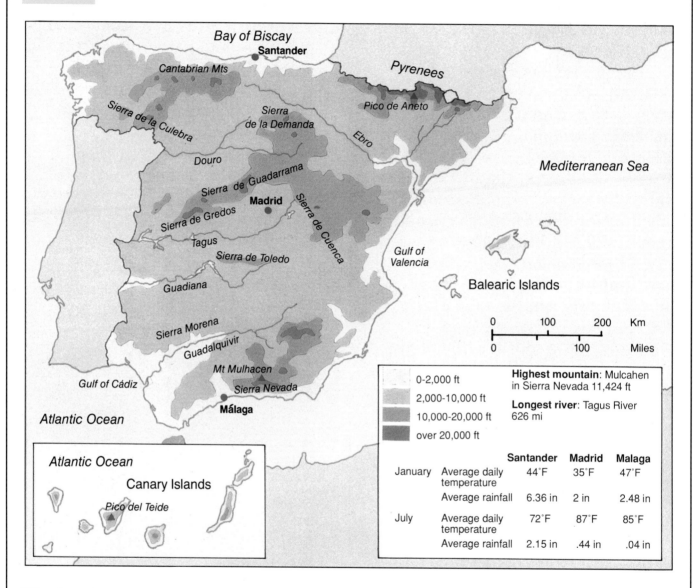

		Santander	Madrid	Malaga
January	Average daily temperature	44˚F	35˚F	47˚F
	Average rainfall	6.36 in	2 in	2.48 in
July	Average daily temperature	72˚F	87˚F	85˚F
	Average rainfall	2.15 in	.44 in	.04 in

Highest mountain: Mulcahen in Sierra Nevada 11,424 ft

Longest river: Tagus River 626 mi

The landscape and climate of Spain are probably the most varied in Europe. Much of the center of the country consists of a vast area of tableland called the Meseta. This huge **plateau** is **barren** and can be very cold in the winter but extremely hot in the summer. It is surrounded and crossed by a number of different mountain ranges.

In the Basque region of the north (in the Pyrenees) the mountains are snow-peaked, and the houses resemble Alpine villages. In the northwest area of Galicia (above Portugal) the weather is very wet and the countryside is green and hilly. The northeast is much drier. In the deep south is Europe's driest and hottest region – Andalucia.

Spanish people also live in the Balearic Islands – a group of four large islands (Majorca, Minorca, Ibiza and Formentera), and seven small islands in the Mediterranean, and the Canary Islands. The Canaries are an **archipelago** in the Atlantic Ocean off the African coast. There are seven islands (Gran Canaria, Lanzarote, Fuerteventura, Tenerife, La Palma, Gomera and Hierro) and six uninhabited islands.

Just over half the Spanish coastline borders the Mediterranean Sea. The region has some of the most consistently good weather in Europe. As a result more foreign tourists visit Spain than any other country in the world.

Above The lush green scenery near Santander on the north Atlantic coast.

Below A farm with a herd of goats in Andalucia, the hottest and driest region.

3 Wildlife

The rare and handsome Mediterranean lynx.

There are nine national parks in Spain and because the country is large compared with its small population, there is still a large variety of wild animals living in the quiet, rural areas. However, because of the extensive developments that have taken place in agriculture in recent years, a number of species are now threatened with **extinction**.

One of the parks, Donana, south of Seville, is the largest European nature reserve covering almost 97,000 sq acres. In this area there are rare animals such as the Iberian mongoose, the endangered Mediterranean lynx (of which there may be only fifteen pairs left in existence) and the world's fourth rarest bird, the imperial eagle. Only fifty pairs of this bird still exist and a quarter of them breed in Donana.

In the summer much of this area of Andalucia, which is in the estuary of the Guadalquivir River, is parched heathland but for the rest of the year it is flooded marshland called the Marismas, which attracts the largest flocks of ducks and geese in Europe. It is a characteristic of Spain that few birds live there permanently.

In the Pyrenees wild boar are hunted for sport as well as food; the izard goat also lives there as well as the endangered Pyrenean ibex and the Pyrenean desman, which is a member of the mole family.

Right The head of the imperial eagle with its large, strongly-hooked beak.

Below A group of Pyrenean ibex goats with their distinctive curved horns.

4 History

The history of Spain is a very complex one. Over the centuries many peoples and cultures have visited and conquered the country. The **Phoenecians**, followed by the Greeks, the Romans, three different German peoples and the **Visigoths** occupied the country. Under 300 years of Visigoth rule Spain became a Christian country. Then in AD 711 came the first **Muslim** attack, which lasted three years and left most of the peninsula under Muslim rule.

The Alhambra Palace, built by the Muslims.

Most of the people of the area accepted being ruled by the Muslims but some either fled across the Pyrenees or lived in the hills and mountains. The unity of the country was destroyed by the Muslim invasion, and small groups of Christians formed themselves into little defensive regions and began to fight back.

Gradually, over 800 years, more and more of Spain was won back, and eventually the Muslims were driven out of the country and back to North Africa from where they had come.

Christopher Columbus and his crew prepare to set sail on their long voyage of discovery.

The last Muslim stronghold was the Kingdom of Granada which surrendered in 1492 to the joint rulers of Spain – Isabella of Castile and Ferdinand of Aragón – after a ten-year struggle. One can still visit the magnificent Muslim palace, called the Alhambra, in Granada.

On October 12, 1492, in the same year that the Muslims were finally driven out of Spain, Christopher Columbus and his crew – with the support of the King and Queen of Spain – landed on what is now the Bahamas. The Spanish discovery and conquest of land caused disputes between the King of Portugal and Ferdinand and Isabella of Spain.

Pope Alexander VI drew a vertical line on a map of the world as it was then known, stating that all the land discovered to the west of it was to belong to Spain and all the land to the east was to belong to Portugal.

Within a few years, the early explorers were replaced by conquistadores – soldiers of fortune who conquered the great and ancient civilizations of the Americas, overpowering their peoples and stealing their gold and land. By 1550 many of the major cities of Latin America had been established as Spanish land, and gold and exotic foods were being shipped back to Spain.

Above The War of Spanish Succession. Opposers of the Bourbons attack Barcelona.

Over the next three centuries (until the end of the eighteenth century) Spain was ruled by the Hapsburgs, and then by the **Bourbon** kings who won the War of Spanish Succession (1702-13). However, in 1808, Spain was invaded again, this time by the French, led by Napoleon. This shook the Spanish Empire. Within two years all the different countries that had been established in Latin America began wars of independence in order to break free from Spanish rule. The French occupation did not last long. After the French were driven out with British help, there were civil wars over who was the rightful heir to the throne.

After the death of Ferdinand and Isabella in the early 1500s, Spain came under the rule of the **Hapsburg** kings. While Ferdinand and Isabella came close to unifying the country during their rule, it was not until 1580, during the rule of Philip II, that the country became finally united. Portugal was part of the united country but in 1640 the Portuguese rebelled. They defeated the Spaniards at the Battle of Montes Claros and finally became an independent nation.

Above General Franco, Spain's dictator from 1939-75.

The **monarchy** was replaced in 1873 by the establishment of the First **Republic**, but it lasted less than a year. The monarchy returned until 1931 when the Second Republic was declared. In 1936 a counter revolution broke out and for the next three years the country was locked in a civil war in which over 600,000 people were killed. General Francisco Franco, a **fascist**, won and ruled the country as a dictator until 1975. After his death Spain once again became a monarchy when Juan Carlos I was crowned king.

The huge stone cross near Madrid, in memory of those who died in the Civil War.

Important dates

900 BC	Celtic, Phoenician, Greek and Carthaginian invasions and colonization.
200 BC	Beginning of Roman occupation.
AD 400	Germanic invasions.
711	Muslim invasion from North Africa.
1300s	Main period of Christian reconquest of Muslim Spain and establishment of Kingdoms of Castile and Aragon, as the dominant political forces.
1474-1516	Ferdinand and Isabella nominally unite Castile and Aragon thus creating the beginnings of the modern Spanish state.
1492	European discovery of the Americas resulting in the beginning of the Spanish Empire.
1580	Portugal annexed to Spain.
1640	Portugal achieves independence.
1702-13	War of Spanish Succession.
1713	Beginning of Bourbon monarchy in Spain.
1808-14	French occupation of Spain in the Napoleonic Wars.
1873-4	First Spanish Republic.
1898	Loss of last of the Spanish colonies of Cuba and the Philippines.
1931-39	Second Spanish Republic.
1936-39	Spanish Civil War.
1939-75	Dictatorship of General Francisco Franco.
1975	Accession of King Juan Carlos.
1978	Approval by national referendum of current democratic constitution.
1982	Spain joins NATO.
1986	Spain joins the EEC.

5 The people today

Above *A girl dressed in a regional costume for a festival.*

Left *Men gathered together at a street market in Seville.*

Continental Spain is divided into seventeen regions, which are then divided into forty-seven **provinces**. Four major languages are spoken in the country – Castilian (the major language which is usually referred to as Spanish and is also the language of Latin America), Catalan, Basque and Galician. During Franco's rule Spaniards were not allowed to speak anything other than Castilian. Since his death the other languages have resurfaced, and today over 9 million people (over one-quarter of the population) speak a **colloquial** language in addition to, or instead of Castilian.

Today, Spain still has very strong regional differences and the people in different areas are fiercely independent – particularly in the Basque region and Catalonia.

The Spanish **economy** has always been largely rural with many people earning a frugal living working on small farms. During the second half of this century, however, things have changed enormously. During the 1950s and 1960s many people left the countryside, particularly the poor areas such as Andalucia and Galicia, to go to cities such as Madrid, Barcelona and Valencia. Others have emigrated, especially to France and West Germany. Many people also move regularly to the coast to work in tourism, Spain's largest industry.

One effect of this movement of people has been the building of new highrise apartments in the outer **suburbs** of the largest cities. At the same time, regions such as Estremadura and Old and New Castile are now more sparsely populated than at any time since the Middle Ages.

Children going to school in the city of Valencia.

6 Cities

Madrid is the capital of Spain and has a population of over 3 million people. In 1561 Philip II decreed that the Spanish court should be based in one place, and Madrid was chosen despite the fact that the city possesses few natural resources. It is neither near a **navigable** river nor by the sea. Madrid's one advantage is that it is positioned in the geographical center of a country that to this day is still divided into strongly independent regions.

Madrid used to be a very beautiful city and the Prado, the country's most important national museum, is located there. There were many other fine buildings, beautiful parks and wide tree-lined **boulevards**. Unfortunately, since 1956, Madrid has experienced more property development than any other Spanish city, and many of the buildings and parks have been destroyed. These have been replaced by housing projects and office buildings.

The tree-lined boulevard called the Ramblas *in Barcelona.*

Above Buildings in Madrid. El Corte Ingles *is the largest department store in Spain.*

Left A busy shopping area in Seville.

The second most important city is Barcelona, which has a population of two million, and is situated on the Mediterranean coast. This city is the capital of Catalonia, and is particularly famous for its magnificent *Ramblas* avenue and its beautiful buildings – some of which were designed by the internationally famous architect Antoni Gaudí. Barcelona is also important because, while it is one of the most heavily industrialized cities in Spain, it is also a center of **commerce** and culture, the arts and sports. Other large cities include Valencia, Seville, Zaragoza, Málaga, Bilbao and Murcia.

7 Life in the country

In past centuries the vast majority of Spanish people lived in villages in small rural communities. Because the country is so large (and the population size relatively small) these communities often lived very far apart from each other. Because of poor road communications they led an isolated life and needed to be self sufficient.

In the past all villagers lived as extended family units (grandparents, parents, children and, eventually, grandchildren all living together in the same house). Everybody, from grandparents down to quite young children, did the daily chores and worked in the fields. The families that live in the villages today still lead a similar lifestyle, except that the interiors of their houses have usually been modernized.

A farmer working in a vineyard in a small, country village.

Children are expected to help on family farms.

Electricity and running water now operate in all but the most remote villages, and most families have modern domestic **amenities** and a car. In all but the smallest villages the roads are now paved. Nevertheless, farming is still hard and constant work, and many children are expected to help their parents seven days a week.

Most villages have a church at their center, and the larger ones have a general store, perhaps a baker and a mechanic, and maybe a bar. A particularly sizeable village may have its own school. Villagers are unlikely to travel far from home unless they are going to a weekly local market, going to celebrate a *fiesta* (or festival) in a local village, or going to work in a nearby town.

The pattern of family life is changing though, particularly with young parents who are successful but still want to live in the country. Increasingly they are moving out of villages, where the houses may be hundreds of years old, and are building themselves brand new, modern houses on the outskirts of villages.

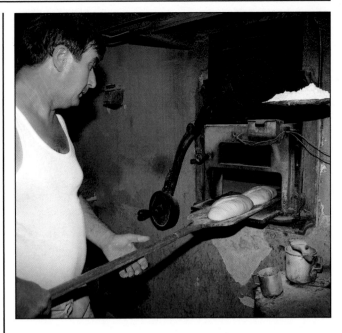

Above *Bread being baked in the traditional way – in a small oven at the village bakery.*

Below *A typical village in Catalonia. This is La Perla near Gerona.*

8 Living in the city

Over the last forty years, large numbers of people have left the villages to find work in the large cities. In Spain today many people live in the huge suburbs of the major cities. Originally having lived in **shanty towns**, many of these people now live in the new highrise apartment buildings.

The children do not have to work as hard as those who still live in the country, but they have less space in which to play. At the end of the day many families all go out walking together. All cities and most towns have a tree-lined street designed for families to walk in. The beautiful *Ramblas* in Barcelona is over a mile long and is very famous. During their walk members of the family discuss the day's events and also meet other friends along the way.

As a result of the rapidly increasing wealth of the country there is also a growing middle and professional class and their lifestyle is extremely comfortable. In July or August the whole family goes on vacation together, usually to the coast or to the mountains.

The whole family returns home at lunchtime to eat a meal together.

There are five mealtimes in a typical day. *El desayuno* is an early breakfast which consists of a hot drink and perhaps some bread and jam. At 11:00 am *el bocadillo de las once* is a kind of second breakfast consisting of a ham or sausage sandwich. *La comida* (lunch) is a long meal eaten at around 1:30 pm and, while many schools provide this meal, families like to return home to eat together if it is at all possible. *La merienda* is a snack meal, sometimes a chocolate sandwich, which children have when they return home from school; and *la cena* is dinner which the whole family eats together as late as 9:30 or 10:00 pm at night! This means that children generally go to bed very late in Spain.

Above *A modern house in a development in the suburbs of Seville.*

Below *Apartment buildings near Barcelona.*

9 Education

Above Children in the playground of a school in a suburb of Valencia.

Left Children working in the classroom at a state school in Cuenca.

In recent years education has improved enormously in Spain, and knowledge is something that is highly prized. Nursery school is supposed to be universal but since nearly half of the schools charge tuition, it means that many of the poorest children do not receive this earliest stage of schooling. However, 9 out of 10 children receive at least one year of nursery school before they go to elementary school.

Since 1970 schooling has become **compulsory** for all children from the age of 6 to 14. Public school education is free for everyone, but in fact one-third of the children go to private schools, which charge tuition, and one half to religious schools, most of which are private.

Because lunch can last a long time, school can finish as late as 5:00 or even 6:00 pm. Children used to have to go to school on Saturday mornings, but in the past few years the *semana inglesa* (English week) has been introduced to give children free time on weekends.

At fourteen, children choose to take one of two sharply divided courses of study. One course follows a very academic path and after four years can lead to university entrance exams. The other course involves a compulsory two years providing a general introduction to **vocational courses**, followed by an **optional** two years engaged in specialized vocational training.

There are a large number of universities in Spain and they too maintain the distinction between academic and practical work. The oldest university is Salamanca which was founded in 1218, and the largest is the Complutense in Madrid which has over 90,000 students. Altogether there are over 700,000 students studying in the Spanish higher education system.

Left Part of Salamanca University which is the oldest university in Spain.

Below A postgraduate student, working in the university at Seville.

10 Shopping and food

A stall in the indoor market in Barcelona selling candy, nuts and preserves.

While the village store still survives in Spain today, even small towns now have supermarkets. Towns and cities also have a large range of small specialty stores that sell a great variety of food. Hams and sausages hang from the ceilings, and on the floor open sacks display grain, chick peas and beans for sale.

However, the most popular place for food shopping for all Spaniards is the market. In the countryside markets move from small town to small town according to the day of the week. In the cities the huge covered markets are open every day.

Bread is eaten with every meal and as there are five mealtimes in the Spanish day huge quantities of bread are bought. Cakes, chocolates and pastries are extremely popular and outside the *pastelería* (cake shop) one can often see people studying carefully what they are going to buy.

The food that people eat varies a great deal across the country but *tapas*, a specialty of Andalucia, are very popular throughout Spain.

Above The flea market held every Sunday morning in Madrid.

Right Women shopping for fruit and vegetables at a market in part of Valencia.

Tapas are eaten in special *tapas* bars while people are having a drink. These bars often have a choice of as many as twenty *tapas*, which are dishes of all kinds of cooked food served in tiny sized portions. The choice includes potato dishes, Spanish omelets, mushrooms and a wide range of meat and seafood dishes.

Other famous dishes originating in Spain include *paella*, which is a rice based dish from Valencia that usually includes shellfish, mussels and other seafood but can also include chicken and rabbit; *gazpacho*, a tomato based soup from Andalucia, served ice cold; and *tortilla*, which is an omelet usually made with onions and potatoes.

11 Sports and leisure

The Spaniards love sports, especially soccer, which is the most popular sport. Outside of Spain, Real Madrid is probably the most famous Spanish team since they won the European Cup five times in succession when the competition first started. The world's richest soccer club is Barcelona, which is based at the fabulous Nou Camp Stadium.

However, the sport for which Spain is most famous is bullfighting, and its history goes back for hundreds of years. Bullfights take place late on Thursday and Sunday afternoons during the summer months. Also famous is the festival week held in Pamplona in July when bulls are released in the street and young men risk injury and even death by running with them.

The Basque game of pelota, which we call jai alai, is another ancient sport. It is played by a group of men who use their hands, a bat or a wicker basket (called a *cesta*) to hurl a ball against a wall. They take turns throwing and receiving the ball. The game is one of the world's fastest and most strenuous.

Spain is very famous for its bullfighting.

More recently golf has become extremely popular, partly because of the number of tourists who go to Spain on golfing vacations and partly because of the international success of a Spaniard who is considered by many to be the world's greatest player – Seve Ballesteros. Since the international success of Manuel Santana and Maria Casals, tennis has become very popular. Other favorite sports are bicycling, sailing, basketball and skiing.

In 1982 Spain hosted soccer's most **prestigious** competition – the World Cup – and in 1992 Barcelona will be the host of the Olympic Games, which is a great honor for the country.

Above Children practicing basketball in a park in central Barcelona.

Below Seve Ballesteros, one of the world's finest professional golf players.

12 Religion

The Christian religion of Spain has always been fiercely Roman Catholic. Protestantism and other religions were not able to gain a foothold until after Franco's death. Catholicism was strong due to the strength of feeling against Muslim rule. In 1480, the Spanish **Inquisition** was set up. This was a kind of law court which tried to ensure unity of the Catholic faith, often by brutal methods. It was fiercely opposed to anyone who disagreed with it. The **Jesuit Order** was also set up to preserve the Catholic faith.

The Inquisition was finally suppressed in the 1830s but its work had ensured that there was no religious freedom in Spain – for centuries Protestantism, Judaism and Islam were outlawed. Even before the establishment of the Inquisition by Ferdinand and Isabella, Jewish people had to live in *aljamos* (walled ghettos) within the cities so that their beliefs and culture could not spread.

The Roman Catholic Church is still very important in Spain, although there has been freedom of worship since 1978. There are Spanish Protestants, a third of whom live in Catalonia, but ninety percent of the population are Catholic. Every town and village has a church, usually quite a sizeable one. Many have beautiful statues inside, often made of gold and decorated with jewels. The cathedral at Seville built over 500 years ago is the second largest cathedral in the world.

Priests are very important people in Spain. They lead the service at christenings, weddings and funerals, give advice and listen to confession. They are unmarried and live near the church. Spain also has many nuns who often work as teachers and nurses in schools and hospitals.

Left The main entrance to the Gothic cathedral in Barcelona.

Left The monastery of Monserrat, which is a very important center for pilgrimages.

Below The holy shrine at Monserrat – the famous Black Madonna.

Many homes have a small crucifix and a small statue of the Virgin Mary. These statues can be seen everywhere in Spain, in homes factories, offices and schools. Spain also has some of the most revered **shrines** of the Catholic religion – at the monastery of Montserrat outside Barcelona, and at the Church of St. James at Santiago de Compostela. Thousands of people go on **pilgrimages** every year along the old pilgrim road to the church of St. James to pray on July 25.

13 Festivals

Left A float carrying effigies of the Madonna and Child in Fuengirola on the Costa del Sol.

Below A penitent dressed for the Easter procession.

Christenings, first communions, saints days and *Diá de la Patrona* (the day of the Protective Virgin) are all important days in the Spanish year. Christmas and New Year are extremely important occasions but the largest events take place at Lent and Easter.

At these times many cities have huge festivals and processions, the most famous of which is held in Seville. On Palm Sunday processions move through Seville's narrow streets. Large floats are carried by men called penitents, who are dressed in long robes and tall pointed hats. The floats often show scenes from Jesus's life, or carry a statue of Mary amid candles and flowers. A band plays music and someone may sing a *saeta*, a sad song about Jesus's life. The processions last long into the night and children stay up late to join in the festivities.

The Thursday following the eighth Sunday after Easter is the *fiesta* of Corpus Christi. The streets are covered with flowers. Along the streets there are long processions, each for the town's own saint. People believe that the saint looks after its own town and people. At a *fiesta*, children dress up in national costume and spend the day singing and dancing to bands in the street. Later the town bells ring, fireworks explode and everybody dances.

Above *A child dressed in traditional white lace for the Easter procession.*

Right *The beautiful flower displays in the streets of Malaga at the fiesta of Corpus Christi.*

14 Culture and the arts

Above A statue of the writer Miguel de Cervantes. In front of him are two of the most famous characters from his writing – Don Quixote and Sancho Panza.

Left A church designed by the architect Antoni Gaudí.

Spain has an extremely rich artistic heritage. The literature of the country is one of the oldest in the world. The *Poem of the Cid*, one of the great medieval epics was written around AD 1140. The great writers of the golden age of Spanish writing in the late sixteenth and early seventeenth century include Miguel de Cervantes and the playwright Lope de Vega. Cervantes wrote the world famous *Don Quixote*, one of the world's first novels, in which the hero has many adventures with his trusty servant Sancho Panza.

Over the centuries there have also been many great Spanish painters, sculptors and architects including Diego Velázquez, El Greco, Francisco de Goya, Antoni Gaudí and, in the twentieth century, Pablo Picasso, Salvador Dalí and Joan Miró.

In music there have been some great twentieth-century classical composers such as Manuel de Falla and Joaquín Rodrigo, but probably the most internationally famous form of Spanish music, singing and dancing is flamenco. Originating with the gypsies in the deep south of Andalucia in the nineteenth century, the music has a strong Muslim influence and wonderfully expresses both the pain and pride of the people's experiences of poverty, oppression and love.

Spain also boasts many fine classical and popular musicians and performers. These include the sopranos Victoria de los Angeles and Montserrat Caballé (who recently recorded a song with Freddie Mercury from the rock band Queen), the baritone Plácido Domingo, the popular singer Julio Iglesias and classical guitarist André Segovia.

A Flamenco dancer and musicians entertain an audience in Seville.

15 Farming

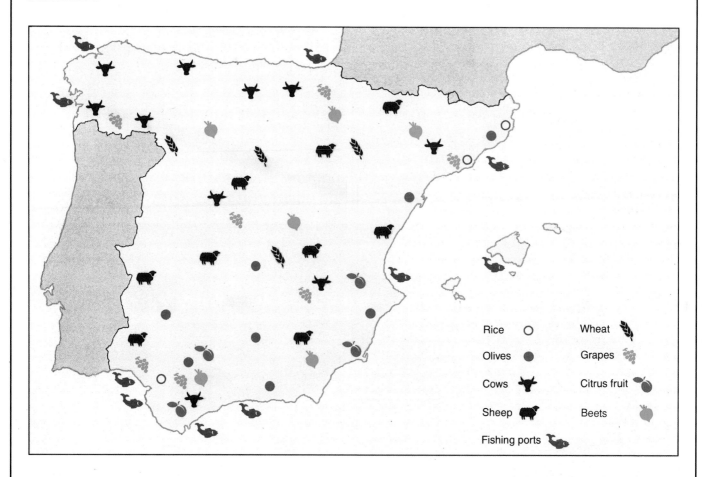

Rice ○   Wheat
Olives ●   Grapes
Cows   Citrus fruit
Sheep   Beets
Fishing ports

As is to be expected in such a rural country, Spain is a huge producer of food and is one of Europe's largest **exporters** of foodstuffs. The country has the largest expanse of vineyards in the world and is the third highest producer of wine. It also has the world's largest area of olives. About half a million tons of olive oil are produced each year, as well as olives stuffed with all kinds of delicacies or preserved in brine.

Spain also produces enormous amounts of fruit, a large proportion of which are exported – especially citrus fruits (oranges, lemons, grapefruit). Pomegranates and avocados are grown in the southern and Mediterranean areas, and apples, pears, plums, peaches and melons are grown in the north and northeast.

The Spanish diet is largely made up of tomatoes, onions, garlic, herbs, chick peas, beans, peas and cereals, which are all grown in great quantities. Meat is also a very important part of most Spanish cooking. Pork, lamb and veal are very popular, as are all the meats used to make sausages and pâtés.

Spain's fishing fleet is among the largest in Europe, and fish is eaten everywhere, particularly in Galicia which produces excellent fish. Spain does not produce a lot of dairy goods so milk and butter production are low, and apart from the Basque region, cheese is not an important part of the diet.

Right Fishermen in Rosas harbor preparing to take their nets out to sea.

Below A farmer using mules to plow a steep olive grove in Andalucia.

16 Industry

Spain's most important mineral resources are coal, iron ore, copper, mercury, zinc and lead. The country also produces large amounts of cement, sulphuric acid, cork (of which it is the world's largest producer), cotton and wool yarn. Many of the richest sources of minerals are now exhausted and the country is having to develop more intensive extraction methods in weaker source areas.

However, since the 1950s Spain has experienced a rapid industrial development. This is due to the movement of rural communities to the cities. As a result, the country now has large and extensive manufacturing industries.

Traditionally, the major industrial centers were based in the Basque country and Catalonia, but now most of the cities have large factory areas. Nevertheless, not all regions of Spain contain heavy industries, and five of the seventeen provinces of Spain (Barcelona, Madrid, Valencia, Biscay and Oviedo) produced nearly half of the country's national output.

Above Spain produces a wide variety of pottery and ceramics for the tourist trade.

Left Leather is made into an assortment of useful accessories.

Main exports:	Food and agricultural products; raw materials, iron ore, coal; manufactured goods; textiles.
Main imports:	Petroleum, raw cotton, animal products, vegetable oils.

The principal manufactured goods include textiles, chemical products, shoes and other leather goods, ceramics, sewing machines and bicycles. Spain builds ships and has a large car-assembly manufacturing industry owned by foreign companies; it also has a small domestic motor industry which produces the national car – the SEAT. Nevertheless, one of the largest industries in Spain is undoubtedly tourism.

Tourism

Many tourists come to Spain to enjoy the beaches and the very fine weather.

Spain is probably one of the few countries in the world that has more annual visitors than it has inhabitants. In 1988 well over 45 million people visited Spain, and they came from all over the world, especially from Britain, West Germany, The Netherlands and Scandinavia. Northern Europeans in particular are attracted to Spain because it has some of the best weather in Europe, is relatively cheap and has developed its tourist industry to meet the needs of visitors.

Most of these tourists go to stay in the Mediterranean coastal resorts on the Costa Brava, Costa Dorada, Costa Blanca and Costa del Sol. Others go to the Balearic Isles, particularly Majorca, Minorca and Ibiza, or to the Canary Islands, where the weather is the finest. Before the 1950s these resorts were quiet, untouched rural areas, but now they consist largely of endless rows of high-rise hotel and apartment buildings facing the sea along with restaurants, bars and discos.

Above A modern hotel on the Costa del Sol.

Less than a mile inland from the sea, however, the old and traditional Spain, which has changed little over the centuries, can still be found.

Some tourists like to visit the ancient and historic cities of Barcelona, Gerona, Seville, Granada, Toledo, Segovia, Burgos, and Córdoba. Others enjoy packaged tours so that they can see the beautiful and extremely varied landscape of inland Spain and the less developed north and west Atlantic Coast.

Many tourists also visit Spain in the winter, either to enjoy the mild weather on the coast or to go to the many recently developed ski resorts which have become very popular in the last few years.

In the tourist resorts there are many restaurants and bars that cater to tourists.

18 Transportation

Spain has only recently developed efficient and modern forms of transportation. Progress was slow because Spain has few navigable rivers (there are only seven sizeable rivers in this massive country); large sections of the country are mountainous; and the sparsely spread population has made the development of highways and railroads a slow and expensive undertaking.

It was not until 1974 that an air shuttle link between the two major cities, Madrid and Barcelona, was opened, and not until the later 1970s that many highways were built.

Today there is air service across the country and a fairly good highway system exists, although in some rural areas the roads are still unpaved. There are also a few rural areas where the villagers use donkeys to ride on and to carry their produce to the local market.

Both Madrid and Barcelona have subways and there is an extensive railroad system across the country. However, many of the train services are slow by European standards with the exception of some express services and the famous train called the *Talgo*.

A Boeing 727 belonging to the national airline, at Barcelona airport.

Left Spain has been slow to improve its railroads but in recent years the system has been greatly modernized.

Below Passengers using a local bus to get around town.

The *Talgo* is a modern Basque-designed and Spanish-built train. It is an extremely comfortable, air-conditioned express with excellent restaurant service and often video screenings. Its most notable feature, however, is that it is the only train that crosses directly from Spain into the rest of Europe. Other trains must stop at the border since Spain and Portugal have a railroad track that is wider than the gauge used in the rest of Europe. The *Talgo* solves this problem by having adjustable wheels that can change from one gauge to the other.

19 Government

After 36 years of dictatorship, General Franco died on November 20, 1975. Two days later Juan Carlos came to the throne of Spain. He has been very important in making sure that a politically democratic and much freer system was introduced into the country. A new **constitution** was prepared and passed in October 1978 by the *Cortes* – the Spanish parliament. The constitution proved to be popular when a **referendum** of the people was held in December 1978.

The constitution established what is called a **parliamentary monarchy**. Also, there is no longer an official religion, the death penalty has been abolished, the voting age is reduced to eighteen and the armed services – historically a very important force in Spanish political life – have been given a very limited role.

Above *An advertisement for regional elections in Catalonia.*

Felipe González, who has been prime minister of Spain since 1982.

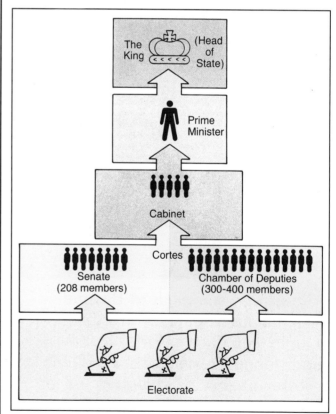

A diagram showing the structure of the Spanish government.

The most important part of the constitution is that it has brought about the development of a **federal** structure for the country. This means that a single province or group of neighboring provinces can make up an **autonomous community**. Each one has a president, a governing council, a legislative assembly, and a supreme court.

In Madrid the prime minister of the central government, Felipe González, is still responsible for many key areas such as foreign policy, but the overall result is that in fewer than ten years one of the most highly centralized nations in the world has been divided into 17 regions each with its own flag, capital city, president and democratically elected assembly.

Above King Juan Carlos and Queen Sophia of Spain.

The Royal Palace in Madrid.

Facing the future

Spanish warships. Spain is a member of NATO but outside its military command.

Spain has changed dramatically over the last fifteen years and it looks as though this process is going to continue, at least in the near future. Politically the country is much more directly involved in European and world politics than it was under Franco. Spain finally joined the **North Atlantic Treaty Organization** (NATO) in March 1982 and the EEC in January 1986.

In 1987 the first Spaniard was elected to become the Director General of the United Nations Educational, Scientific and Cultural Organization (UNESCO).

In the early 1970s Spain had the fastest growing economy in the western world, and the growing success of the country was reflected in the growth of Barcelona. Today, Spain's economy is more similar to

Above A film set near Almeria. "Spaghetti Westerns" are filmed here. It is one part of a thriving film industry.

Below The building of the stadium in Barcelona for the 1992 Olympics.

that of other European countries.

The 1992 Olympics will be held in Barcelona, and both the city and the region are undertaking a massive building program. At the same time there is a development of cultural and social life. A whole new group of young fashion designers based in the city are developing a unique style. Barcelona is becoming one of the most important centers of book publishing in Europe. There are also many young and ambitious people working in the Spanish film industry and for the rapidly expanding television system of the country.

Spain's future looks hopeful, full of exciting changes and new ideas.

Glossary

Amenities Agreeable facilities and services.

Archipelego A group of islands.

Autonomous community A group of people who are to some extent self-governing but live in a country with laws that apply throughout the land.

Barren Infertile; unable to support plant life.

Boulevard A wide tree-lined road in a city, often used as a promenade.

Bourbon A member of a French royal family that ruled in France, Italy and Spain during periods spanning many centuries.

Colloquial Familiar or regionally local speech, or language that is not usually used in formal situations.

Commerce Trade. The exchange of goods and services for money.

Compulsory Required. Describes something that must be done.

Constitution The set of basic principles and rules on which the government of a country is based.

Democratic Having a system of rule in which the population elects people to represent them in a government.

Dictatorship A country or government in which the ruler, or dictator, has absolute power.

Economy The financial organization of a country and its resources; also the production and distribution of wealth within the country.

Empire A group of countries ruled and dominated by another country.

European Economic Community (EEC) An association of twelve Western European countries that tries to coordinate policies on agriculture, industry, trade and taxes.

Export To sell goods to a foreign country.

Extinction Dying out, as when a species of plant or animal no longer exists.

Fascist Someone with extreme right wing political beliefs; often someone in a military system who believes in aggressive nationalism.

Federal Describes a union of states having a central government.

Hapsburg The German royal family who ruled over the Holy Roman Empire from 1440-1806. They also ruled countries such as Austria, Spain, Hungary and Bulgaria.

Inquisition Established in Rome by the Pope in 1231, the Inquisition was set up to combat opposition and witchcraft in the church and to enforce unity. It was introduced into Spain in the 1400s and cruelly treated Jews, Muslims and Protestants.

Jesuit Order A very strict section of the Roman Catholic priesthood.

Monarchy A nation or state headed by a king or queen.

Muslim A follower of the religion of Islam.

Navigable Deep and wide enough for travel by boat.

North Atlantic Treaty Organization (NATO) A group of countries in North America and Europe that have signed an agreement to defend each other in the case of war.

Optional Left to personal choice; not required.

Parliamentary monarchy A system that has a democratic ruling party and a king or queen as head of state.

Phoenicians An ancient people who lived in what is now Lebanon, Syria and Israel. They arrived in that area in 3000 BC and were a powerful seafaring nation of traders and colonizers in the Mediterranean for 2,000 years.

Pilgrimages Journeys made by religious people to a shrine or church that is considered important in their religon.

Plateau A flat area of land that is high above sea level.

Prestigious Recognized as having or giving prestige, respect or fame in some field.

Provinces Regions within a country.

Referendum The placing of an issue or law before the people so that they can vote on it.

Republic A country in which the voters elect officials to run the government and make the laws.

Shanty towns Houses on the outskirts of cities that are built of waste materials.

Shrines Sacred or holy places.

Suburbs The outer districts of a city.

Visigoths A branch of the Goths who came from Germany. From AD 4 to AD 711 they ruled over Spain and much of Europe.

Vocational courses Educational courses to train a person for a particular job.

Books to read

Anderson, David, *The Spanish Armada* (Hampstead, 1988).

Banyard, Peter, *The Rise of the Dictators: 1920 – 1939* (Franklin Watts, 1986).

Lye, Keith, *Europe* (Gloucester, 1987).

Lye, Keith, *Passport to Spain* (Franklin Watts, 1987).

Matthews, Rupert, *The Voyages of Columbus* (Bookwright, 1989).

Meltzer, Milton, *Columbus and His World* (Franklin Watts, 1990).

Pellicer, Maria Eugenia D., *Spanish Food and Drink* (Bookwright, 1988).

Picture acknowledgments

All photographs were taken by David Cumming with the exception of the following:
J.Allan Cash Ltd 15, 22 (top), 25 (both), 30 (bottom), 31 (bottom); Bruce Coleman *cover*, 5, 7 (bottom), 8 (left), 9 (both); Greg Evans Picture Library 18 (right), 30 (top), 31 (top); Mary Evans Picture Library 12 (top); Christine Osborne 35 (bottom); Photri 11; Popperfoto 12 (bottom); Topham Picture Library 18 (left), 27 (bottom), 42 (left), 43 (top); Wayland Picture Library 22 (bottom).